Schaumburg Township District Library

130 South Roselle Road

Schaumburg, Illinois 60193

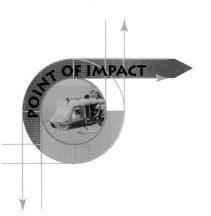

POINT OF IMPACT

The Fall of Saigon

The End of the Vietnam War

MICHAEL V. USCHAN

Heinemann Library
Chicago, Illinois

Customer Service 888-454-2279

Visit our website at www.heinemannlibrary.com

Produced for Heinemann Library by Discovery Books Limited
Designed by Sabine Beaupré
Illustrations by Stefan Chabluk
Originated by Ambassador Litho Limited
Printed in Hong Kong

06 05 04 03 02
10 9 8 7 6 5 4 3 2 1

Library of Congress Cataloging-in-Publication Data
Uschan, Michael V., 1948-
  The fall of Saigon : end of the Vietnam War / Michael V. Uschan.
      p. cm. -- (Point of impact)
Includes bibliographical references and index.
  ISBN 1-58810-555-5 (lib. bdg.)   ISBN 1-4034-0072-5 (pbk. bdg.)
  1. Vietnamese Conflict, 1961-1975--Vietnam--Ho Chi Minh City--Juvenile literature. 2. Vietnam--History--1975---Juvenile literature. 3. Ho Chi Minh City (Vietnam)--History--Juvenile literature. [1. Vietnamese Conflict, 1961-1975.] I. Title. II. Series.
  DS559.9.S24 U86 2002
  959.704'3--dc21
                              2001003479

Acknowledgments
The author and publishers are grateful to the following for permission to reproduce copyright material:
Corbis, pp. 4, 5, 6, 7, 8, 10, 11, 12, 13, 14, 15, 16, 17, 18, 19, 20, 21, 22, 23, 24, 25, 26, 27, 28, 29.

Cover photographs reproduced with permission of Corbis.

Special thanks to Robert Carpenter for helping us improve the accuracy of this book.

Every effort has been made to contact copyright holders of any material reproduced in this book. Any omissions will be rectified in subsequent printings if notice is given to the publisher.

Some words are shown in bold, **like this.** You can find out what they mean by looking in the glossary.

Contents

Surrender in Saigon

The surrender of South Vietnam

Just after midday on April 30, 1975, a new flag was raised over the presidential palace in Saigon, the capital city of South Vietnam. The president, Duong Van Minh, had surrendered to North Vietnam, bringing an end to the Vietnam War.

Some residents of Saigon were afraid that they would be killed when the North Vietnamese took over their city. These people are trying to get into the United States embassy in the hope that they will be flown to safety by helicopters.

Fleeing Saigon

Elsewhere in the city, helicopters were landing and taking off from the rooftops, carrying people to safety. Thousands of Saigon residents, fearful for their futures after the defeat, rushed into the United States **embassy** to join American citizens who had clambered onto the roof. In fear of being left behind, people fought brutally to get on the helicopters. It was the largest helicopter **evacuation** in history. In about eighteen hours, starting on April 29, the aircraft carried nearly 7,000 Americans and South Vietnamese to ships waiting offshore.

North Vietnam wins

The dramatic helicopter flights were just part of the chaos taking place on the final day of the Vietnam War. At the same time, thousands of soldiers from North Vietnam were rolling into Saigon in tanks and trucks to capture the city.

When Saigon fell, it was clear that the North Vietnamese and the **Vietcong,** their **allies** in South Vietnam, had won the war. As a result, North and South Vietnam were **reunified.**

Victorious North Vietnamese soldiers enter Saigon in April 1975 as the city falls and South Vietnam surrenders.

A war that shook the world

The Vietnam War had raged for twenty years and had taken the lives of more than two million people. It caused problems and conflict around the world. North Vietnam had received support from its allies, the Soviet Union and China. Soldiers from other nations, including over 50,000 Australians, had helped South Vietnam. South Korea had also sent thousands of soldiers to fight on behalf of South Vietnam. Over the years, the U.S. sent nearly three million soldiers to support South Vietnam, an action that changed both countries forever.

A Nation Yearning for Freedom

Colonial powers

In the 19th century, Great Britain, France, Germany, and other strong nations were colonial powers—they took control of weaker countries. Settlers from the colonizing country took land in the **colony.** They hired local peasants to work for them for very low pay. The colonizing country also took control of the colony's **natural resources.** By using these resources and selling them, the colonizing country became richer and more powerful. Wealth and power allowed them to colonize even more countries.

Life in rural Vietnam is based around rice farming. In some ways the country remains the same as it has been for centuries.

A French colony

In the second half of the 19th century, France seized control of Vietnam and two neighboring countries, Laos and Cambodia. France governed these countries in southeast Asia as a colony they called French Indochina.

Vietnam's main natural resource was coal. It was also a farming nation, and most of the Vietnamese people were peasant rice farmers who lived in small villages.

Unhappy Vietnamese

Vietnam was part of the French empire from 1883 until 1954. The French made the laws, profited the most from the **economy,** and **exploited** the Vietnamese people.

Early in the 20th century, many Vietnamese, angry about being ruled by France, began to demand independence. One of them was Nguyen Singh Cung (or Nguyen That Thanh). He later became known as Ho Chi Minh, which means "he who **enlightens.**" He believed in nationalism, or the right of citizens to rule their own country without interference.

European colonialists in the 19th century often used the strength of their superior armies and weapons to take over other parts of the world. Here, the French enter Hanoi, the capital of Vietnam.

Request for rights

In 1919, at an international peace conference after World War I, Ho Chi Minh asked for some rights and freedoms for the people in Indochina. France preferred to keep ruling its colony as it had in the past, however, and although President Woodrow Wilson supported **self-determination** for all nations, Ho Chi Minh's request was denied by the U.S. and other countries. He became a communist in 1920 and continued to push for reforms for his country.

VIETNAM'S LONG HISTORY

Vietnam is an ancient land. It first emerged as an independent kingdom called Nam Viet in about 200 B.C.E. For much of its history, however, it was dominated by bigger and stronger nations. China, its powerful northern neighbor, conquered Vietnam in 111 B.C.E. and ruled it for more than a thousand years. The country became independent again in 939 C.E., when the Ly dynasty drove out the Chinese.

Vietnam Defeats France

Ho Chi Minh declares independence

In 1940, during World War II, the French surrendered control of their **colony** to Japan when the Japanese invaded Indochina. Ho Chi Minh then saw a chance to free his country. He created the League for the Independence of Vietnam, also called the Vietminh. The Vietminh began fighting the Japanese and successfully resisted the invasion. On September 2, 1945, Ho Chi Minh gave a speech that proclaimed his country's freedom. He borrowed a key phrase from the American Declaration of Independence by saying, "all men are created equal."

Battle of Dien Bien Phu

The French, who had never treated the Vietnamese as their equals, wanted to regain control of Vietnam. In 1947, Ho Chi Minh and the Vietminh began to fight French forces for their independence. With financial and military support from the United States, France expected a short conflict. They were repeatedly surprised, however, by **guerrilla** attacks. The Vietminh hid in the jungle, ambushed French troops, then disappeared back into the jungle. Finally, in May 1954, a decisive battle ended in Dien Bien Phu, a village in northwest Vietnam. Over 10,000 French soldiers surrendered there after a massive siege.

French soldiers pulled out of Hanoi, the capital of North Vietnam, in 1954, after the Vietnamese won the battle at Dien Bien Phu.

France decided to withdraw its forces from Indochina after the bitter defeat.

A country divided

Ho Chi Minh thought Vietnam had finally won its independence and would be free of foreign interference. However, the conflicts in Vietnam had become part of the Cold War. This was a battle for world supremacy after World War II between the **communist** Soviet Union and the **capitalist** United States. Ho Chi Minh's dream of greater freedom for his people was shattered.

When the United States and other nations met in Geneva, Switzerland, in July 1954, the group approved the Geneva Accords. The agreement called for a temporary division of Vietnam into two nations: North Vietnam and South Vietnam. Ho Chi Minh became the leader of communist North Vietnam and established Hanoi as the capital. Saigon was established as the capital of capitalist-supported South Vietnam where a Vietnamese general named Ngo Dinh Diem became leader. The Geneva Accords also required that an election was to determine the leader of a **reunified** Vietnam in 1956.

This map shows Vietnam and its neighbors Laos and Cambodia, also once part of French Indochina. When Vietnam was split, North Vietnam was backed by another neighbor, the large communist nation of China.

The U.S. Gets Involved

Fighting communism

Americans in the 1950s feared **communism** because they felt it denied people freedom. American leaders believed in containment, the need to keep communism from spreading. Between 1950 and 1954, the U.S. gave France $2.6 billion to battle communism in Indochina.

When France was defeated in 1954, President Eisenhower decided that the United States must continue opposing communism in Vietnam. The U.S. officially supported Ngo Dinh Diem, president of South Vietnam, and from 1954 to 1963, gave South Vietnam about $1.7 billion in aid and military training and weapons.

John F. Kennedy, soon to be president, visits President Eisenhower at the White House in 1960. Eisenhower had been supporting South Vietnam with soldiers and money for several years. Now the conflict was in Kennedy's hands.

Meanwhile, Ho Chi Minh built up the **economy** in North Vietnam. He redistributed the land among peasant farmers, often by pushing landowners off the land or even imprisoning them. Many people fled from North Vietnam to South Vietnam when the Geneva Accords split the country.

No fair election

In 1956 it was time for Vietnam to **reunify** under an elected government. In North Vietnam Ho Chi Minh was elected president. Ngo Dinh Diem, however, refused to hold an election, saying he did not believe a fair election was possible.

War begins

Ho Chi Minh decided to reunify his country by force. He needed the land in South Vietnam, which was better for farming. Also, South Vietnam was getting aid from the U.S., and North Vietnam was suffering even though the Soviet Union and China were giving them aid. Ho Chi Minh reorganized the Vietminh army, which was joined by supporters in South Vietnam. The combined group was called the National Liberation Front of South Vietnam, or **Vietcong.**

Starting in 1955, the U.S. sent "military advisors," or soldiers, to support South Vietnam and train the Army of the Republic of Vietnam (ARVN). South Vietnam was not united behind Ngo Dinh Diem, however. There was growing unhappiness with the way he was ruling the country.

THE FREE WORLD

After World War II, U.S. leaders were afraid that if one country in Southeast Asia became communist, others would follow. This was called the domino effect. After he was elected president in 1960, John F. Kennedy claimed South Vietnam was important as "the cornerstone of the free world in southeast Asia."

Chinese leader Mao Zedong (left) was a powerful communist who supported Ho Chi Minh (right). The two leaders are shown at a banquet held in Ho Chi Minh's honor in China in 1955.

A Guerrilla War

The Vietcong

The **Vietcong** fought a **guerrilla** war. In guerrilla warfare, there are no large armies meeting on the battlefield. Instead, small groups of soldiers act on their own, making surprise attacks. The Vietcong understood the importance of surprise. They lived as rural villagers, which made it difficult for the South Vietnamese army to know who was Vietcong and who was not.

They took control of the countryside and, from their rural **strongholds,** fought the South and engaged in terrorism. They exploded bombs in major cities, where the South Vietnamese and their **allies** were in control. It was not hard for the Vietcong to target their enemies in the cities and army encampments. The Vietcong captured and held more than 58,000 national, local, and village officials. They also killed more than 36,000 other officials.

Ngo Dinh Diem, a Roman Catholic, persecuted **Buddhists,** like these monks drying rice outside their temple. Some Buddhist monks even burned themselves alive in protest of restrictions Ngo Dinh Diem placed on their religious activities.

South Vietnam weakens

In spite of the growth in American aid to the South, the **communists** were winning the battle for Vietnam. By 1962, the Vietcong's fierce guerrilla warfare had given them control of much of the nation's rural area.

The Vietcong's success was also partially because Ngo Dinh Diem governed South Vietnam so brutally and badly. He gave a lot of power to his family members, and many of his government officials were corrupt. They stole money and supplies that should have gone to help people. Generally, the South Vietnamese hated the way Ngo Dinh Diem ruled their country. On November 1, 1963, several generals from his own army captured and assassinated Ngo Dinh Diem and then took control of South Vietnam.

A mother hides with her baby in a canal bank near her village in South Vietnam. The South Vietnamese soldiers passing by have just reclaimed the village from Vietcong guerrillas.

Another assassination

Only a few weeks after Ngo Dinh Diem was overthrown and killed by his army, President Kennedy was assassinated in Dallas, Texas. Kennedy's tragic death meant that the vice president, Lyndon B. Johnson, became president. He took on the difficult duty of determining the United States' continued involvement in Vietnam.

A SOLDIER'S DUTY

A Vietcong soldier wrote this to his girlfriend during the Vietnam war: *"Before, I did not know what it was like to kill a man; now that I have seen it, I don't want to do it anymore. But it is the duty of a soldier to die for his country, me for our fatherland, the enemy for his. There is no choice."*

More Help from the U.S.

President Lyndon B. Johnson

The newly sworn in President Johnson wanted to save South Vietnam from **communism,** but the **Vietcong** grew stronger and stepped up their actions after Ngo Dinh Diem was killed. Johnson decided that the U.S. had to do more to help South Vietnam.

A ship crammed with American soldiers arrives in Vietnam. By 1968 there were about 536,000 Americans fighting in the Vietnam War.

Officially, he was limited to sending military advisers. These "advisers" went on information-gathering missions. They were told to fire back if fired upon. Officially, they were only advisers to South Vietnam. In reality, they were fighting in the war. Under President Johnson, this type of war activity grew.

On August 3, 1964, three North Vietnamese patrol boats fired on the U.S. destroyer *Maddox*. The ship was gathering information in the Gulf of Tonkin, off the coast of North Vietnam.

The event gave President Johnson reason to call for more power to fight the war. Congress passed the Gulf of Tonkin Resolution in response, which Johnson signed on August 11. The resolution did not declare war, but it allowed Johnson to **escalate** the role of the U.S. by sending more troops and "to take all necessary measures to repel any armed attack against the forces of the United States."

Operation Rolling Thunder

The U.S. began bombing North Vietnam from the air in March 1965. The attacks were known as Operation Rolling Thunder. Many bombs were made of **napalm,** which caused fires and destroyed huge areas of jungle and many villages.

OTHER PARTICIPANTS

The United States was not the only nation that sent soldiers to help South Vietnam. Members of the South East Asia Treaty Organization (SEATO) also fought in the Vietnam War. These are the numbers of soldiers other countries had there in 1968.

Australia	7,660
New Zealand	520
Philippines	1,580
South Korea	50,000
Thailand	6,000

By the time Operation Rolling Thunder came to an end in 1968, the United States had dropped three times the number of bombs dropped in World War II. Yet the Vietcong remained strong.

No End in Sight

Search and destroy

During the American **escalation** from 1965 to 1968, ground forces performed **search and destroy** missions. Americans set up base camps in the jungle, and select soldiers would move out from the base camp into the jungle, searching for and killing **Vietcong.** The Vietcong hid very well in the thick jungle, though. They also disguised themselves and hid in local villages. To force the Vietcong out, U.S. soldiers moved villagers out and declared the villages "Free Fire Zones." The villages were then destroyed.

Death and deception

Powerful airplanes, superior weapons, and helicopters that could rush soldiers into battle helped American forces kill a large number of **communist** soldiers, but the Vietcong stayed strong. The U.S. began issuing false lists of the number of killed enemy soldiers to make it appear as if the U.S. was winning the war. Meanwhile, the number of American fatalities grew rapidly.

A door gunner on a "Huey" helicopter is ready to open fire if he spots any Vietcong. Helicopters were used in search and destroy missions.

In Hue, Vietnam's cultural and religious center, about 2,800 civilians were gunned down during the Tet Offensive, and the city was left in ruins. Here, American **Marines** in Hue take cover behind their tank after being fired upon by the Vietcong.

The Tet Offensive

From January 27 to February 3, 1968, a temporary truce was held to honor Tet, the Vietnamese New Year. Ho Chi Minh, ignoring the truce, launched a surprise **offensive** on January 31. About 70,000 Vietcong and North Vietnamese soldiers struck 36 towns and cities throughout South Vietnam. The attacks, known as the Tet Offensive, lasted several weeks.

In only a few days, the North Vietnamese army and the Vietcong took over several capitals and the U.S. **embassy.** U.S. and South Vietnamese forces eventually defeated the attackers, but the offensive had destroyed many villages and cities.

MY LAI MASSACRE

The Vietcong did a good job of hiding among local villagers and creating confusion. Frustrated and scared, American soldiers sometimes mistakenly shot civilians. On March 16, 1968, in a village called My Lai, between 175 and 200 unarmed villagers, including children, were killed by American soldiers who suspected the entire of village of helping the Vietcong. The victims were innocent, and the officer in command was later convicted of murder. A villager who survived the massacre at My Lai later said, *"It's why I'm old before my time. . . . I won't forgive as long as I live. Think of the babies being killed, then ask me why I hate* [the Americans]*."*

An Unpopular War

The war on television

The Vietnam War was the first war to be shown on television. Rather than relying on written reports, people saw for themselves what was happening in Vietnam. News shows aired images that showed the destruction of cities and villages and women and children running for their lives. In January 1968, people were stunned by pictures of the incredibly violent Tet **Offensive.** It showed that U.S. officials were not providing all of the facts when they claimed that the **communists** were being defeated.

Antiwar protesters

At first, Americans were united in helping South Vietnam. As America's involvement in the war **escalated,** however, the public became divided. Those who supported the war were called "Hawks" and those who opposed the war were called "Doves." As the years went by, more and more Americans—especially young Americans—felt their country's involvement in Vietnam should come to an end. The **draft** was one reason for this opposition.

A priest gives comfort to a dying **Marine** after an attack by North Vietnamese soldiers. People around the world questioned why American lives were being lost in Vietnam.

The draft required young men to join the military and fight in Vietnam even if they disagreed with the war. As the news made very clear, thousands of drafted soldiers were being killed, and many people decided to voice their anger about it.

Antiwar protests spread through American universities in 1965. Over the years, the Dove movement grew stronger and the organized protests increased. There were marches and demonstrations in major cities and smaller demonstrations on campuses across the country.

Protesters are shot

In May 1970, U.S. troops were still in Vietnam, and protests were widespread on college campuses. The protests turned to tragedy when, at Jackson State University in Mississippi, two students were killed and several others were injured as police began shooting in an attempt to stop the protest. Another student died at the University of Wisconsin when a bomb placed by war protesters exploded at the wrong time. The most well-known protest tragedy occurred at Kent State University in Ohio. National Guardsmen were called in to end a protest there and opened fire on the student protesters. Four students were killed and several others were injured.

A crowd gathers in Washington, D.C., to oppose the Vietnam War. Demonstrators hold up a large peace sign, which became a familiar symbol of protest during the war years.

From Battles to Peace Talks

Richard Nixon takes over

President Johnson became very unpopular because of his administration's policies of increasing American presence in Vietnam. He decided not to run for reelection in 1968. Richard Nixon, who promised to bring American troops home, won the presidency.

Vietnamization

Nixon's plan to bring American soldiers home was to make South Vietnam strong enough to defeat the **communists** without the support of American forces. He called it "Vietnamization." Nixon continued to send Americans to Vietnam because his plan required a dramatic increase in U.S. aid to South Vietnam in the form of military equipment and advisers. Ten months passed before he began pulling American troops out of Vietnam. Meanwhile, about 10,000 American soldiers died during Nixon's first year as the president of the United States.

The main negotiators between the U.S. and North Vietnam were Henry Kissinger (right) and Le Duc Tho (left). Many people believe that it is because of Kissinger that the U.S. finally succeeded in withdrawing from Vietnam.

Americans withdraw

In 1969 there were almost half a million Americans fighting in Vietnam. Nixon promised that in July of that year, 25,000 soldiers would come back to the United States. He promised to bring another 85,000 home by the end of the year and all American troops out of Vietnam by 1971 at the latest.

By the end of 1971, the number of Americans in Vietnam had dropped to 160,000. South Vietnamese soldiers were doing most of the fighting while the U.S. Air Force provided air support and continued bombing attacks. The Air Force attacked communist **strongholds** in neighboring Cambodia and Laos, cutting off supplies and refuge for the communists.

Peace talks

Another of President Nixon's policies was to pursue peace talks with North Vietnam. In May 1968, under President Johnson, American representatives had first met with North Vietnam officials in Paris to negotiate a peaceful end to the war. The talks continued on and off for several years, both publicly and secretly.

During this time, the fighting continued and sometimes even intensified. In spite of this, a peace agreement was finally reached on January 27, 1973. The Paris Peace Accords were signed by North Vietnam, South Vietnam, the U.S., and the **Vietcong.** The agreement called for a complete cease-fire and for the U.S. military to withdraw completely from Vietnam. It also said that foreign military activity should stop in Laos and Cambodia. For the future, it was agreed that Vietnam should receive **economic** aid and that North and South should work together for **reconciliation.**

Captain Michael Kerr arrives home to his family in 1973. He had been a prisoner of war in Vietnam since his airplane was shot down in 1967. Nearly 600 American prisoners of war held in Vietnam were released as a condition of the 1973 Paris Peace Accords.

The Fall of Saigon

After the peace agreement

Unfortunately, the only part of the peace agreement that was upheld was the U.S. military withdrawal. The last American troops left Vietnam on March 29, 1973, but the fighting in Vietnam continued. Each side blamed the other for breaking the peace agreements.

The fighting continues

After the U.S. withdrew, the South Vietnamese army tried to fight off the **communists** who had remained in place. The U.S. continued to give South Vietnam money and equipment. However, South Vietnam was unable to resist the **guerrilla** forces. For two years neither side made substantial gains. In January 1975, though, the collapse of South Vietnam began. Attacks on their northern and coastal regions caused the South Vietnamese to retreat farther and farther south as the North Vietnamese gained ground.

South Vietnam's last day

On April 29, North Vietnamese soldiers surrounded Saigon and fired artillery shells into the city. The explosions announced South Vietnam's last day.

On a rooftop in Saigon, an American government employee helps a line of terrified Vietnamese into a helicopter that will fly them out of the city.

In the previous few weeks, American officials in Saigon had **evacuated** 120,000 South Vietnamese. These **refugees** feared the communists would kill them or put them in prison for having supported the South Vietnamese government. As the fall of Saigon loomed, the U.S. also evacuated 20,000 American citizens, mostly government employees and their families. The last people to leave were taken by helicopter from the roof of the U.S. **embassy** and other sites to ships anchored in the South China Sea. "The roof of the embassy was a vision out of a nightmare," said American government employee Frank Snepp.

Refugees crowded into the port at Saigon as the city fell to North Vietnam. They hoped to be taken to safety by American troops.

Ho Chi Minh City

The evacuation ended when North Vietnamese communist troops entered Saigon. On April 29, South Vietnamese President Duong Van Minh ordered his troops to stop fighting. The war was over and the communists had won.

Saigon got a new name and a new government that day. The city would now be called Ho Chi Minh City after the legendary leader who three decades earlier had started fighting for Vietnam's independence and who had died in 1969.

DEATHS IN THE VIETNAM WAR

North and South Vietnamese civilians	over 1,000,000
North Vietnamese and **Vietcong** troops	about 900,000
South Vietnamese troops	about 200,000
American civilians and troops	about 58,000
Australian troops	about 500

Vietnam After Reunification

North and South reunited

In April 1976, the remaining government in South Vietnam surrendered. When the North Vietnamese took over the South, they combined the two parts of Vietnam into one country. On July 2, 1976, the two Vietnams were officially **reunified.** The new nation was named the Socialist Republic of Vietnam and Hanoi was named the capital.

Reeducation camps

Many people fled South Vietnam because they thought the **communists** would kill those who had opposed them. As it turned out, there were no mass executions as had been feared. However, thousands of people were sent to "reeducation" camps and forced to support communism. Many people in the camps were treated inhumanely. Some were even tortured and killed.

All over Vietnam, from tiny villages to large cities, homes were destroyed. In Saigon, seen here after a bombing attack, thousands were left homeless.

War's devastation

The war had caused unbelievable damage in Vietnam. Bombs had flattened large sections of major cities. American airplanes had also sprayed more than 1.8 million gallons (72 million liters) of herbicides—chemicals that kill plants—to destroy the thick foliage of the rain forest that hid communist soldiers and the rice crops that fed them.

The herbicides had further, lasting effects. They polluted large areas of farmland, making them unusable for years. The chemicals—such as Agent Orange—also caused fatal diseases in those who were exposed to them, including the American soldiers who had done the spraying.

There were other dangers that also had lasting effects. Thousands of land mines that had been buried by both sides continued to explode, killing and injuring people.

A long recovery

The war shattered Vietnam's **economy.** It is still one of the world's poorest and least advanced nations. Most Vietnamese live in poverty and their systems of education, health care, and technology are far below those enjoyed by other people throughout the world.

Millions of South Vietnamese people became **refugees.** Thousands, known as the "Vietnamese boat people" because they arrived in boats, fled to Hong Kong, but there was nowhere to house them except in camps such as this one.

VIETNAM'S NEIGHBORS

The fall of Saigon was a turning point for Vietnam's neighbors, too. The government of Cambodia surrendered to the communist-led Khmer Rouge at the same time as communists were occupying South Vietnam. In nearby Laos, communists soon took control without any bloodshed.

The U.S. After the Vietnam War

First loss

The fall of Saigon was a symbolic defeat for the United States that was seen on televisions around the world. Not only had its military forces failed to win in Vietnam, but Saigon's surrender was a political disaster. U.S. policies in Vietnam had not maintained a noncommunist government in the South. It was clear that political and military leaders had failed to work as a team.

For a time after the Vietnam War, the U.S. avoided any large-scale **intervention** in foreign conflicts. Americans did not want to repeat what they saw as a large and costly mistake.

Economic problems

The U.S. spent about $167 billion on the Vietnam War. The United States borrowed billions of dollars to cover these costs. The debt caused **economic** problems and unemployment for several years.

President Richard Nixon appeared on television in 1970 to tell the nation why he had ordered U.S. attacks on Cambodia, Vietnam's neighbor. Over the course of the Vietnam War, many Americans began to question their leaders' decisions.

Loss of faith

Vietnam was the first "television war." Americans watched the horrors occurring in Vietnam on television, while the government assured them that the U.S. was winning. Many people later felt the government had misled and even lied to them.

In 1973 Congress passed the War Powers Act. It required the president to inform Congress within 48 hours of sending troops into action overseas. Both houses of Congress had to approve the action within 90 days, or else the troops would have to leave. Americans hoped the War Powers Act would prevent unnecessary bloodshed in the future. The Vietnam War taught Americans to carefully evaluate their government's response to world events.

Other effects

Rather than a parade, soldiers returned home to bitter disregard and even open hatred. Many Americans wrongly blamed the **veterans** for U.S. involvement in the war. Finally, in 1979, President Carter officially recognized the veterans' service in the war by declaring the first Vietnam Veterans' Week.

The war also changed the U.S. population. More than one million southeast Asians, including about 700,000 Vietnamese people, fled **communism** by emigrating to the U.S. Many **refugees** escaping communist rule sought a better life in the U.S.

DAMAGE DONE

Former Defense Secretary Robert McNamara helped plan the Vietnam War. Years later, he admitted the war had harmed the U.S. He said, "*By the time the United States finally left South Vietnam in 1973, we had lost 58,000 men and women; our economy had been damaged by years of heavy and improperly financed war spending; and the political unity of our society had been shattered, not to be restored for decades.*"

Veterans of the Vietnam War gather every year on Veteran's Day at the Vietnam Memorial in Washington, D.C. There they are honored for their service and remember those who died in the war.

The World After the Fall of Saigon

In 2000, Vietnam and the U.S. signed a trade agreement, something that never would have happened during the Cold War. As a result, American businesses are building factories such as this one in Vietnam.

The effect of a communist victory

Contrary to the domino theory, the fall of Saigon did not lead to **communism** sweeping through southeast Asia. But the victories in Vietnam, first against France and then against the U.S., did give hope to other nations that were being forcibly ruled. Citizens of **dictatorships, colonies,** and later even communist countries, increasingly fought for freedom.

Worldwide opinion of the U.S.

Many smaller nations continued to look to the U.S. for support in protecting their freedom, but indecision by the world's most powerful nation affected many countries. In the 1990s, the U.S. hesitated to respond to the conflict in Yugoslavia, and many Americans opposed **intervention.**

On the other hand, after the Vietnam War, many nations became suspicious of American intervention abroad and remained so. American **allies** in Europe, for instance, had never supported American involvement in Vietnam, and the United States's relationship with China continued to be unstable.

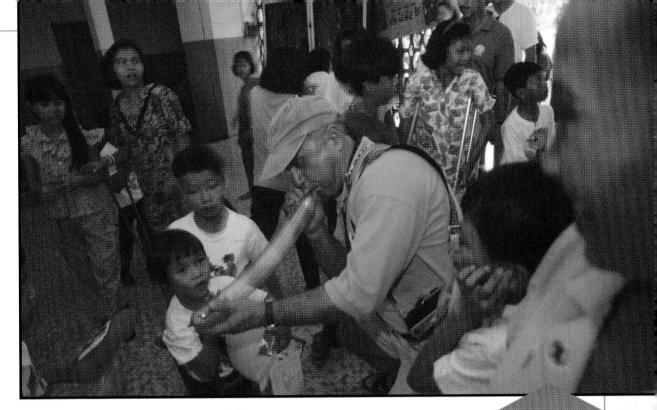

The end of the Cold War

The Vietnam War was an extension of the Cold War between the United States and the Soviet Union. After the fall of Saigon, the Soviets continued giving Vietnam about $1 billion in **economic** and military aid each year. The huge amounts of money spent by the Soviet Union to support Vietnam and other communist nations helped to weaken its own economy. The resulting economic problems, among other factors, led to the Soviet Union's collapse in the early 1990s. This in turn brought about the end of the Cold War.

The United States and Vietnam

The breakup of the Soviet Union eased American fears about communism, making it easier for the U.S. and Vietnam finally to resume peaceful relations. In November 2000, President Bill Clinton became the first president to visit Vietnam since Nixon's 1969 visit. Clinton proposed the two countries should work together for a better future. "Once we met here as adversaries [enemies]," he said. "Today, we work as partners."

An American **veteran** of the Vietnam War visits this orphanage in Ho Chi Minh City (formerly Saigon) twice a year. As well as entertaining the children there, he brings money and medicine that they need.

Timeline

1883–1954	Vietnam ruled by France as part of French Indochina
1945	September 2—Ho Chi Minh declares Vietnam independent
1946–1954	Vietminh fight French forces for control of Vietnam
1950–1954	U.S. provides military and economic aid to French to fight **communism** in Indochina
1954	May 7—communist forces defeat French at Dien Bien Phu July 21—Geneva Accords divide Vietnam into North and South
1955	February 23—first U.S. military advisers sent to Vietnam April—fighting begins as **Vietcong** and North Vietnamese try to overthrow government of South Vietnam October 26—Ngo Dinh Diem declares himself president of South Vietnam without elections
1960	November—John F. Kennedy elected president of the U.S.
1962–1963	President Kennedy greatly increases U.S. military presence in Vietnam
1963	November 1—South Vietnamese President Ngo Dinh Diem assassinated November 22—John F. Kennedy assassinated and Lyndon Johnson becomes president
1964	August 2—American destroyer *Maddox* attacked in Gulf of Tonkin August 4—Congress approves Gulf of Tonkin Resolution
1965	February 7—President Johnson orders bombing of North Vietnam
1968	January 30—North Vietnamese and Vietcong launch Tet **Offensive** March 16—between 175 and 450 unarmed civilians killed in My Lai Massacre May—First peace talks November—Richard Nixon elected president of the U.S.
1969	Vietnamization begins First withdrawal of American troops from Vietnam September 3—Ho Chi Minh dies
1970	Four students killed in antiwar protests at Kent State
1973	January 27—Paris Peace Accords signed March 29—last American troops leave South Vietnam Congress passes War Powers Act
1975	April 30—Saigon falls and South Vietnamese government surrenders to communists
1976	July 2—North and South Vietnam reunited as Socialist Republic of Vietnam
2000	Trade agreement between Vietnam and U.S. November—President Bill Clinton visits Vietnam

Glossary

ally   friend or supporter in a conflict

Buddhist   follower of the Asian religion of Buddhism, which teaches people to aim for enlightenment and goodness

capitalist   economic system in which private individuals own property and make economic decisions

colony   nation or region ruled by a separate country

communism   economic and political system in which government controls the economy and citizens have common ownership of property and resources

dictatorship   country ruled by a dictator, a person who takes complete control often without being elected

draft   legal requirement for people to join their country's military forces; in place in the U.S. since the Revolutionary War

economy   resources, such as goods and services of a nation, and the system of money that controls resources

embassy   office and residence of an ambassador, the person who represents his or her government in a foreign country

enlighten   to help show the truth or make something clear

escalate   to increase in stages

evacuation   getting people out of a particular area during an emergency

exploit   to use or take advantage of people, usually unfairly or cruelly

guerrilla   soldier who fights or attacks as part of a small independent group

intervention   getting involved in affairs of other countries

Marine   member of the United States Marine Corps, a branch of the military forces

napalm   sticky chemical substance that causes things to burn

natural resources   useful materials found in the land, such as fuel (coal, gas, and wood), valuable metals (iron and gold), or water

offensive   organized attack on an enemy

reconciliation   act of getting back together or becoming friends again

refugee   person forced to leave his or her home

reunify   to join back together

search and destroy   missions to find and kill enemy soldiers

self-determination   right to make decisions about one's own life and country

stronghold   place where a group can hide out and store supplies

veteran   person who has served in a war

Vietcong   communist-led army of South Vietnamese formed to fight South Vietnamese government

Further Reading

Ashabranner, Brent K. *Their Names to Live: What the Vietnam Veterans Memorial Means to Americans.* Brookfield, Conn.: Twenty-First Century Books, 1998.

Gay, Kathlyn. *Vietnam War.* Brookfield, Conn.: Twenty-First Century Books, 1996.

McCormick, Anita Louise. *The Vietnam Antiwar Movement in American History.* Berkeley Heights, N.J.: Enslow Publishers, 2000.

Index